Nuggets of Wisdom

Bob Sizemore
Catholic Counselor

with

Ronda Chervin
Professor, Speaker, Writer

En Route Books and Media, LLC
Saint Louis, MO

⊕*ENROUTE*
Make the time

En Route Books and Media, LLC
5705 Rhodes Avenue
St. Louis, MO 63109

Cover credit: Sebastian Mahfood

ISBN-13: 978-1-956715-96-5
Library of Congress Control Number: 2022949385

Table of Contents

Introduction

by Bob Sizemore

By "nugget," I want to convey that within this nugget of a problem there is actually an opportunity for growth.

by Ronda Chervin

I first met Bob at Holy Apostles College and Seminary where both of us were teaching. I liked him for his friendly smile and hilarious jokes ready to amuse us in the dining room. But I got to really appreciate him only when he agreed to be a crisis counselor to me. At the time, the life of one of my adult daughters was threatened by lymphoma.

I found Bob's insights into my problems about facing the probable death of my daughter were augmented by his general insights about life.

I also enjoyed the novels he was writing. So, even after I left the area of the seminary, we kept in contact. From time to time, I phoned him for instant advice.

A few months ago, Bob phoned: "Would you consider helping me write a book of nuggets of wisdom?"

"Of course! Nothing to lose and everything to gain."

TOWARD
A HAPPIER DAILY LIFE

Forgiveness

Bob: Forgiveness is a very delicate flower. Unfortunately, we don't nourish it enough but, rather, stunt its growth. Of course, when this happens, everybody loses: ourselves, those we don't forgive, and the Christian community we live in.

Ronda: I like to distinguish between forgiving those who personally hurt us and forgiving everyone who did wrong. Forgiving a thief who stole a car is different from trying to forgive Hitler for the holocaust of the Jews.

Bob: Here, I want to concentrate on personal forgiveness. I think most people would agree forgiveness is a wonderful thing. However, they would also say, not here and not now. The source of this resistance is the ego. It wants to be right all the time. Of course, it can't be right all the time, and that's why we have forgiveness. In fact, if we are honest with our past, we would have to admit sometimes, "How could I have been so right (ego) but at the same time so wrong?"

I have met people for the first time and immediately I didn't like them. However, over the years I have come to realize that they had qualities that were instructive for me and very admirable.

Forgiveness has no time boundaries. It might happen right now, five years from now, or just before the end of our lives.

My biggest act of forgiveness occurred with the coming death of my father from cancer. My mother and father divorced when I was three and my sister was two. He became a negative figure in our lives because he would only show up to see us on occasion.

About ten years ago, my father came back to New Haven to say goodbye to friends and family. My sister, Beverly, and I were faced with a dilemma. Even though we still felt like the aggrieved parties all of these years, he was still our father and soon we would no longer see him.

Given the finality of the situation, Beverly and I decided to forgive him. I came to two conclusions about him that I had not considered before.

1. He lost his mother and father at an early age and was left on his own. There was no parenting there. I had to admit that I could not have survived the aloneness any better than he did.

2. As a Christian and a lay Franciscan, I had a mental image of his leaving his world on a passenger train to wherever.

I saw that I had this one opportunity to make things right. So, I forgave him. My sister also forgave him, and we could then both wish him

Godspeed. I forgave him in person as my sister did, for our whole life without a father.

Ronda: How did he react?

Bob: For the very first time he allowed me to hug him. To me, this was a sign of acceptance.

Ronda: My best forgiveness story is this. My husband was brought up in a Jewish family where only women went into the kitchen. I worked to support the family because he was disabled with terrible asthma. I always had to also cook and clean since men of his background usually didn't do such things. At the end of the evening at nine PM after he had sat back watching TV while I marked papers from my classes, he would say: "How about a cup of tea and dessert?"

I would grind my teeth and obediently make the tea and bring out the dessert.

One evening I was at a prayer meeting where the priest insisted that all couples hold hands and totally unconditionally forgive each other for everything that hurt them in their whole marriage.

I grabbed my wedding ring and repeated the words of forgiveness.

When I came back home, my husband opened the door and said: "Honey, you look tired, can I make you a cup of tea?"

I realized later that when the anger went out of my eyes because of forgiveness, he could see the tiredness.

This changed my marriage of twenty-five years from what I would call a B- to a B+.

Bob: What a great story! It shows how forgiveness warms our hearts.

The second story from my life history involves a "coming of age story" on my part. This time, I had to ask for forgiveness which I never accomplished. I have prayed for the person I hurt but have lost track of him over time. In my thirteenth or fourteenth year, I had a run-in with another boy my age, a classmate. He was egged on by a tougher kid who probably wanted me to be humiliated. My opponent, whom I will call Billy, and I met in the old cemetery next to our school.

We faced each other about three feet away with our fists up in the air. I saw Billy, for one brief moment, look back at his handler while smirking. I thought to myself, I am known as a smart student but not as a tough guy. When Billy looked away, I pulled my right fist back and hit him right in the mouth. He fell down backward just sitting on the ground. Then, I hit him again in his chest while yelling at him. He ended up with a chipped tooth.

This was my one and only fight of my life! It put me one up and him one down in our school community. I also was never challenged again by anybody. I felt on top of the world. My ego had emerged to defend my personhood in a very physical way. I feel sorry for Billy and wish we could have made up.

So, in our lives, at the moment of death, we are left with that very unique Christian quality of forgiveness. It is probably the most underused and precious part of the Christian life. If we seek forgiveness from Christ, how could we not forgive all those who wronged us and hope to be forgiven by those we have wronged. God the Father, before we can be with Him in heaven, will probably say to us, "Did you forgive your neighbor as Christ did on the cross?" Let us not forget we are children of God and remain so for eternity as long as we remain open to forgiveness.

For the Reader:

You might want to inscribe here an experience of forgiving and/or asking for forgiveness. Or, you might want to list by initials those you still need to forgive or ask forgiveness from and then pray for the grace to try to do it.

_____

_____

_____

_____

_____

_____

_____

_____

_____

_____

_____

Coping with
Idiosyncracies of Others

Bob: This topic may seem unimportant at first glance, but it has the power over time, like a drop of water hitting our heads every five seconds, to be extremely annoying.

I am talking about the small quirks we all have, which can cause a relationship to fall apart. The main aspect of these habits is that they are not a "big deal," but that's precisely their power.

Ronda: Many wives hate that their husbands don't look up from the newspaper or the TV or, nowadays, the cell phone, when the wife is trying to talk about the problems of her day!

Bob: I am talking about things such as laughing inappropriately, using too many sentences that start with "I" as in I want this or that, calling you by your hated nickname which was given to you by a very angry brother, and repeating parts of your sentences as if they were their own.

Before I give some more concrete examples from my own life, I just want to emphasize that any unwanted or unexpected behavior has the ability to break up marriages and cause divorces. The reason is that person you are talking to has heard and seen these messages so many times, they become the actual messages that drown out what the other person was trying to say. The response by the interrupter is really a coded message that they want to take control.

The husband says, for example, "In our family we always sat quietly at the dinner table." The wife responds, "What a wasted opportunity!"

Many times these "disrupters" can be traced back to our unconscious minds as a form of passive resistance by a child to his parents' demands. The wife loved dinner conversations when she was a child, so she really means that she dislikes how quiet her husband is at meals.

If she would have said, "Don't you realize that I want to hear something interesting from your day at work?" it would be more direct.

The child usually wants to speak and talk about the day but is excluded from doing so by the parents' attitude that he or she should just shut up and let them talk.

I believe that this type of poor communication, which starts in the family, is multiplied many times over in the child's daily and adult life.

Ronda: Oh, I think I am getting it. Many people have told me that they dislike how I always interrupt people when they are talking. So, this probably goes way back to feelings of being interrupted by parents when they were children.

Bob: The anger of the wife in my earlier example when her husband ignores her when she is talking may reach proportions of her wanting to leave him because it triggers every time a feeling of being ignored by her parents.

Ronda: Would such a fantasy or reality of leaving her husband over this seemingly trivial fault really be a defense mechanism?

Bob: The key word is "seemingly." What is small to the husband is big for the wife. What the wife is left with is the fact, in her mind, that he doesn't listen to her, therefore, doesn't love her.

Ronda: Wow! Given so many of these seeming idiosyncrasies, such as the husband's habit of not looking up when his wife is talking to him, how can any close relationship ever work at all?

Bob: Unfortunately, in today's American society, most people are driven by the need for fast actions and conclusions.

Ronda: Oh, as in thinking that if someone goes to marriage counselling for six months their marriages will go from B- to A+?

Bob: It could go up to B+! I believe this desire to rush through almost everything today eliminates the possibility of listening and knowing what's going on in the other person. I see this concretely in funerals. Funerals in my view used to last at least three days where families got a chance to mourn and come together. Today, they are down to one day, and there is a reduction in the ceremony because of cremation. The message is there is no time to mourn together.

Another problem: we associate PTSD, post-traumatic stress disorder, with war. But, it also can happen in families domestically.

Ronda: You mean, for instance, trauma from being sexually abused by siblings or relatives or even parents?

Bob: Not only sexual but also emotionally overwhelming experiences such as witnessing violence in the family or receiving violent responses by parents as a child.

Ronda: Hmmm! Since spanking is now a reason why children can be taken away from their parents legally, was spanking in the past that violent?

Bob: It could be, certainly. A little tap on the behind is different from beatings until blood comes or welts result.

To continue my thread, what happened in Vietnam was very severe emotionally for many soldiers. Therefore, they came home with PTSD, and basically the war continued for them in their heads.

Personally, I know a soldier who came back from Vietnam and was still living that experience at home. He felt so threatened that he slept in bed with a machine gun that he brought back from Vietnam.

Ronda: In terms of idiosyncrasies, such a traumatized soldier might get furious with his wife and children for leaving windows open in the night so that enemies could easily enter.

Bob: The big picture is that PTSD is a domestic problem as well today. We may not sleep with machine guns, but we may sleep with forty-fives under our pillows.

What does all of this mean? It means that all of us need to be listened to, much like all of us as babies need to be nursed by our mothers. Listening is the adult milk of life.

Ronda: How would listening help resolve my example of the husband and wife? Do you mean that a tired husband coming home from a 9 to 5 job and an hour commute has to listen for an

hour to his wife's repetitive stories about her trivial problems?

Bob: Yes, because these problems may be
trivial to the husband but not to her.

Ronda: Point well taken, but if I was a marriage counselor, which I am not, I would suggest
that they have a happy hour first before she
launches into these stories.
I mean there is often a compromise solution
to problems with annoying traits of others rather
than an extreme change.

Bob: I would add, if it wasn't for the annoy-
ance, a counselor or a good friend could never
help you to get to the real problems underlying
the behaviors.

For the Reader:

Think of an example of some seemingly trivial behavior of someone close to you that annoys you and think and pray about insights in Bob's Nuggets that could be helpful in better understanding and improvement. How about asking others what idiosyncrasies of yours annoy them? Then, try to improve.

_____

_____

_____

_____

_____

_____

_____

_____

_____

_____

_____

_____

_____

_____

_____

_____

_____

_____

_____

_____

_____

_____

_____

_____

_____

_____

_____

Peacefulness

Bob: Don't we all long for peacefulness in our lives amidst the everyday chaos? When we are peaceful, we are different persons.

Ronda: Hmmm! Well, I don't long for peacefulness; I long for victory! And I am so seldom peaceful that it's not as if tumult is the occasional interruption of peaceful feels; rather, peaceful feels to me are always like a miraculous sudden grace.

Bob: Well, Ronda, as I continue, I think you will see that you are more peaceful than you think.

Every person has their own idea of what peacefulness is for their individual personality. I also believe peacefulness is like a multi-faceted diamond. There are so many ways to be peaceful if you can just access it.

My experience is that I walk into a new situation and, all of a sudden, I feel totally at one with myself. There is nothing to do but, with all the time available, just be. Peacefulness comes from within and manifests itself in the quietness of this moment. Let me borrow from my own experience.

The first manifestation of peacefulness for me is from an unlikely source. When I see a multicolored "quilt" on a bed, I am immediately drawn to different multi-colored pieces of cloth that some caring person put together, creating both a beautiful piece of artwork and a paradox.

For me, a quilt mirrors completely my whole life. There wasn't a beautiful bedspread, in one piece and one color, given to me to jump start my life. Rather, I had to put my life together by taking pieces of cloth wherever I could find them, to finally convince me that I, too, had made it to a wonderful warm bed and a great night's sleep of my own making. Now, I could look forward to tomorrow and a new day. The paradox, of course, is that life, like the quilt, came together piece by peace. The peacefulness is both in the view of the quilt and in the balance in life that the pieces represent. I and the quilt are one in this moment.

Ronda: This is fascinating because it happens that I have been making knitted quilts or throws most of my life. Now, with a lesser income, I ask others to donate to me their extra yarn, and I make what I call "crazy quilts" for all of my family and friends.

Bob: In a somewhat similar way, I find great peacefulness in meeting someone for the first time who has no agenda but his/her peacefulness to share with me. This person, in sharing his or her life experience, is really guaranteeing that peacefulness is being conveyed so that I can share it with so many other people I meet in my life. To that extent, peacefulness is teaching by a peaceful teacher. My point here is that in order to develop peacefulness in ourselves, we must first be great students.

As a counselor, I never want to be drawn into a client's anger or angst. I am doing my very best when I meet my client at his/her boundary and listen but don't cross the boundary.

Ronda: Well, as a matter of fact, I have always found greater peace going to counselors and spiritual directors, and all of them are ten times more peaceful than I am.

Bob: A third ingredient of peacefulness is silence. How you get your own best silence is your own choice. For me, freshwater fishing, by myself, at a small pond, is very cathartic. Releasing the line with bait or lure on the end and hearing the float first touching the water is a wonderful fishing experience but, also, it has the quality of being a quasi-spiritual experience.

The beauty of the day is in the numerous times I cast out and don't give up. That certainly imitates life. I go through a whole day and sometimes catch nothing. However, I did catch that wonderful feeling of peacefulness.

Ronda: Hmmm! I don't fish, but my most peaceful times are simply gazing at bays, rivers, or oceans.

Bob: When I see my wife, Barbara, or my children, or my grandchildren, after a period of time, there is a tremendous peacefulness when we come together. I believe this is due to the fact that we were all together at one time in heaven before we were born. What a peacefulness to encounter the other who is a part of you already. My wife Barbara and I have been married for fifty-five years. We are each eighty years old. My peacefulness with Barbara comes with the fact that quite often, I can't tell where she begins and I end.

So, too, is peacefulness true with our three children. We knew them intimately when they were babies. Now, each of them is over fifty years old. For each of them, my peacefulness soars when I can say, "I remember when…" This process is doubled when I think about our three grandchildren who are each over twenty years old.

Ronda: I am happy for you, dear Bob, that your experience is so peaceful. I think of family more as a battleground…but there is more about the paradigm of life as a battle in other chapters of your nuggets.

Bob: There is a special peacefulness as I write this summary, whereas many people in reading a good book get "lost" in the drama. I get lost in

my writing itself. There is a peacefulness that em-
anates from my very inner core directly to the
pen I am using. It is a continuous feedback loop.
For me, as a writer, there is an instantaneous
peacefulness that just flows through my whole
being.

Ronda: As the writer of some seventy-seven
books, I can say Amen to that, Bob. I know there
are some writers who write even though they
hate doing it and it is a struggle all the time. But
for me it is easiest thing I ever do.

Bob: So, Ronda, every time you wrote one of
those books you got into your peacefulness even
though you never labeled it as such because for
you, it seems, your definition of peacefulness
would only be total heavenly bliss.

Kind of, the writing is the interruption from
the chronic anger.

Of course, for all Christians and Catholics, there is an ultimate peacefulness in Christ. Every first Saturday of the month, Barbara and I go to a nearby Franciscan church for Mass. Above the altar, there is a huge brown wooden cross that shows Christ spread out and crucified.

As I gaze upon this cross, I am immediately drawn to the cross and am at one with the cross. The peacefulness is immediate and long-lasting. As long as the Mass lasts is as long as I am transfixed. I really feel one with Christ.

Ronda: I was reading an old novel *The Eye of the Storm* by Patrick White - a terrific Australian writer, not a Catholic.

After reading his description of a woman buffeted in a plane during a storm until it diminishes when they come into the eye of the storm I thought:

Holy Mass is our Eye in the Storm. Also, if we are peaceful and gentle and patient we become eyes in the storm for others.

The counselor is often the eye in the storm for his/her clients.

Bob: Indian tribes have two chiefs, a war-chief and a peace-chief…

Horse racing, you have changing strides…if the horse isn't winning by leading with his right foot, the jockey changes him to the left foot. Yin and Yang.

For the Reader:

Write about when you are most peaceful. What insights of Bob Sizemore were important to you?

_____

_____

_____

_____

_____

_____

_____

_____

_____

_____

_____

_____

_____

_____

_____

_____

_____

_____

_____

_____

_____

Simplicity of Life

Bob: Life is actually quite simple. We are born, we live "x" number of years with choices we have made, and then we die.

Ronda: You mean there's no life after death?

Bob: Yes, there is, but I want to focus in this "nugget" on life upon this earth.

The simplicity is in the fact that we have a mind, and we inhabit a body of certain proportions. Most of the people reading this book are not in a state of destitution. We actually have very simple choices placed before us of which we may choose to partake and which will probably take care of our basic human needs.

The problem that enters the picture is in the idea of greed, of wanting more of everything. It would not be so bad if more meant more of good things of life – more exercise, more hopefulness, and more good will. However, this is precisely the point where the train falls off the railroad tracks. We also want more cigarettes, drugs, alcohol, ex-rated movies, fatty foods, etc. Thus begins the slow and steady decline to obesity, breathing problems, heart problems, diabetes, etc.

Along with these triggers of ill health, we have mental issues too – depression, anxiety, OCD, hoarding, and obsessive compulsive behavior. The list goes on and on until one day you find yourself in a hospital with two to four weeks to live. Simplicity suddenly turns into eternity.

But wait! Simplicity is never totally gone if we would declutter our lives of objects and "toys" we thought we could never live without. I like to call this stage of our lives, again, if we choose it, the purification stage.

Standing in the way of this stage is the array of addictions, supported by various media that want people to remain subservient and dehumanized. So, we are left with the autonomous individual seeking simplicity vs. the collective of big business, big media, and computer–driven lives.

A central part of simplicity is knowing when to say "yes" and, more especially, when to say "no." The temptation is always to say "yes," but experience shows us the choices we said we couldn't do without are precisely what we should have said "no" to. In this case, the brightest star in the sky becomes an alluring black hole swallowing up our total individuality.

To make the simple choice, we need time to think not just react. There is no doubt in my mind that a big portion of the problem here is the pace at which we are forced to live or choose to live. The human being is not a machine; it needs time to reflect on decisions. It also needs quiet time to do some long-range planning that will continue to make our lives simple.

Ronda: When I think of simplicity of life, I am always contrasting having too much stuff when the cost of it could go to the poor. They say that what Americans waste in food could feed the whole world…I wish that instead of relying on institutional charities, in every parish, by living more simply, we would contribute much more each year so that there wouldn't be any hungry person or street person – as in some NYC parishes that have a leader street person supervising some of the homeless at night in the Church, etc. etc. etc.

Bob: Perhaps an even bigger question that goes along with simplicity is: does simplicity make for a happier life? All you have to do is talk to retired people. Although retirement means your salary is cut in half, your time to be with your spouse, your family and your friends may indeed be doubled. It is at that point in time that the realization comes into focus: simplicity means better and closer relationships. There is no longer a place to rush off to but just a time to be!

Ronda: Of course, the ideal is having a live spouse and family nearby. Many retired people have none of this and feel lonely and bored.

Bob: I can think of no better example for the need for simplicity than hoarding. The person for various psychological reasons feels the need to accumulate and save both big and small items until that need overwhelms him or her. They are usually left with a very small space in the middle of this accumulation to operate their daily lives. How sad that this person born with a God-given right of freedom is now bound by a lifetime of objects.

Ronda: Nowadays, a distinction is made between hoarders who can no longer function at all and those described rather as clutterers. A hoarder might be someone having no room to even sleep on a bed because it is so covered in clothing, or, worst case, hoarding containers of fecal matter because the toilet is clogged.

Now counselors I know of think that underlying hoarding is loneliness, as in the widow desperately misses her spouse and then keeps all his stuff around the house to make it seem as if he is still, somehow, there.

Bob: But there is still hope. With the help of a counselor, the person is led to throw out or give away anything not needed. Eventually, the house or apartment is "un-covered," and the person can go back to normal living, probably with ongoing counselling.

This lack of simplicity is a matter of degree for people. The important point here is who or what do you invest in – yourself, other people, or things!

The answer is self-evident – we are on this earth to help other people and reach out instead of making a bunker for ourselves to slowly lose our humanity.

Ronda: I love when people by living with only what they need can give a lot to charities and individuals in desperate need.

Now that doesn't mean that everyone out of simplicity should have nothing but material necessities. A piano isn't a luxury for a pianist. But having so much stuff that one can't even find what one needs is surely not living simply.

For the Reader:

What is your experience with simplicity of life as Bob Sizemore describes it? Any experience of de-cluttering?

_____

_____

_____

_____

_____

_____

_____

_____

_____

_____

_____

_____

_____

_____

_____

_____

_____

_____

_____

_____

Healing of Childhood Wounds

Bob: Childhood is a very special time in the lives of adults. Witness the "state" most of us fall into when Christmas comes. The lights, the tree, the candles, and the Christmas bulbs all contribute hypnotically to an altered state of consciousness. That state is a temporary reliving of our childhood for this brief period of time. For many of us, it is a happy time. For many others, it might be a very depressing time.

Ronda: For example, we were poorer than most of the children at our public school. They came in after Christmas showing off beautiful expensive gifts. And we had nothing to show that was comparable.

Bob: This is the one time of the year, not the only time, when our childhood wounds may be rekindled much as embers in a fireplace may have a sudden resurgence.

The difficult thing about talking through childhood wounds is that they are so laden with emotional contents that they once again feel real and affect us accordingly all over again.

Therein lies the problem for adults. They thought they got rid of these negative feelings in their lives, but here they come again!

How do you get rid of them?

Actually, technically, you don't! All you can do is reduce their intensity so that they are no longer giants in your life but actually microscopic.

They are real. They did exist, and they want a voice at the table so they can be heard. The point is these childhood wounds need our help to mourn the situation once and for all.

For each wound, there is a solution. One solution in the now is to remind one's mind that this wound is not just in the past but the distant past.

Ronda: For instance, I might think of all the wonderful presents I got at Christmas for years after that.

Bob: There are, however, some wounds that are so deep-seated that they can only be handled metaphorically.

Ronda: For example, I know a mentally ill woman who was serially raped as a child by her older brothers. Her mother wouldn't believe her.

Bob: So a metaphorical way of handling such a thing might be devotion to Mary, Mother of Jesus and the Church, whom she knows believes everything she tells her.

Let's be clear. We are talking about the healing of childhood wounds. These wounds came into being due to the perception of the child at the time.

An adult would have a greater range of choices due to experiences of day-to-day living. Even something as vicious as rape can put the person on a trajectory to become a counselor to women traumatized by such tragic events. Thus, a childhood incident leads to an adult fulfillment.

Here is a metaphor: the oyster can only produce a pearl when it has some grit in it to develop that pearl. So, too, a bad childhood memory has the potential to lead to a much greater life.

Ronda: My big wound was my father leaving my twin sister and myself when we were eight years old to marry a woman younger than my mother. Years later, in talking about my conversion to the Catholic faith, I would always share that for me becoming a Catholic included finding thousands of men called "Father," the priests, who laid down their lives for us to feed us our celestial banquet, the Eucharist.

Bob: Just as the natural tendency of the body is to heal, so, too, is it true of our emotional, psychological wounds. There are two comments worth noting here. The first is that the person has allowed this wound to fester so long that it has become an integral part of who she is! For example, when someone has been called stupid, that is the trump card they hide behind when challenged to do new things.

The second point I want to make is that the wound, in order to heal, needs a totally different approach. It needs a metaphorical approach. By that, I mean something that causes the mind, especially the unconscious mind, to seek a new path to operate on which excludes the old wound. As one matures, the sudden realization is that stupid is a relative term and that lessens the impact of the original wound. One could see that, say, you could be very smart at tech without getting A's in English grammar in grade school.

Another example, a young woman in childhood may have the wound of being ugly which she herself reinforces every day by looking in her mirror. However, one day, by chance, she enters a local beauty contest, and to her complete surprise wins. Now she is presented with two choices: keep the old wound of ugly or adopt the new image of beautiful with all the ensuing compliments. There is no longer room for ugly, only the brand new sparkling goal of beautiful.

The point is that life will give us opportunities to reverse old wounds if we just seize them and exchange the new for the old.

Another critical point I want to make is that you can't go forward in your life on a negative, only a positive. It's the opportunities in life that really interest the person, not a title that someone has put on us for selfish reasons.

It is especially a place in these times where fathers and grandfathers can interact in a warm, loving way for their children to emulate.

Ronda: Oh, Bob, one of my memories is of a family gathering where there was lots of stress between generations. We opened the monopoly board and had fun for about a half hour until someone accused another of cheating and that one grabbed the board and threw it on the floor and no one ever suggested that game again.

Bob: That shows how far he diverged from the better humorous self into the more critical self. Dr. Jekyll and Mr. Hyde? Both are real. Which one predominates?

Getting back to the positive, let us not forget the grandparents in the game. They get an opportunity to see, maybe for the first time, their children and grandchildren in a whole new caring light. This is precisely the renewal of love that grandparents need; the reassurance that they will be cared for and loved in the future.

Ronda: A grandson-in-law of mine loves to play self-devised family games where he mimics the way each of us talks and acts. It is hilarious and, I now realize, also healing.

Bob: Board games are also learning experiences where you both observe other generations' ways of acting and reacting, and whole new views of people who were not in your awareness.

It brings to mind the whole idea of game theory. Here, my family is present to open themselves to the game. What happens is that the game is so joyful and fulfilling that no one really wants to stop. The big question we were left with is this: "Is the game reality and everything else I do pseudo-reality?"

What we are left with is a "new weapon of choice" in our lives which is humor. With the depression, suicides, murders, etc., going on in our society, humor gives us the ability to go on with our lives and survive another day.

I once wrote a saying that applies here: "humor is the oil for the engine of success, for the friction of stress, and for the wear and tear of ego."

Ronda: One of my daughters used to run family birthday parties where each member drew a cartoon-like picture of the person whose birthday it was, and the others had to guess who had drawn each one.

In my present living situation with a dear friend my own age, after a day that might include some stressful conflicts, ending the day with games of double solitaire is wonderful. Still, I would never think of life itself as a game!

Bob: You may with your Jewish background think life is meant to be a battle, not a game, and if you were to indulge much in the board game it would be a rejection of your whole past.

I'm seeing the game as a paradigm and less stressful. Everything has to do with perception, so if you start with the perception of life as a battle that's how you treat it, but if it is a game, then you free yourself up for much more flexibility in how you operate.

Ronda: Oh, after talking about this battle paradigm, I read something interesting about being a battler, as I certainly am. It is from a novel called *Green Dolphin Street* by Elizabeth Goudge. Here is the passage: "And fighting…is never over; only when you are old it narrows to the battlefield of your own body and soul."

But certainly you don't mean, Bob, that you see yourself not as a counselor and professor but just someone who plays games all your life?

Bob: You're not getting it. That's not what I mean. In board games, others see you in ways you don't see yourself. What this also says is that you have greater choice in your life. You can also have humor, not only battle.

For the Reader:

What is your paradigm of life such as battle vs. game, or....?

_____

_____

_____

_____

_____

_____

_____

_____

FOR SELF-EXAMINATION

How Do I See My Place in the World?

Bob: This is a very intriguing topic which is totally age-related. When we are young, the universe revolves around us. Well, doesn't it?

A tell-tale sign of this is all the "I" statements we make at this time. This stage would also indicate a tremendous desire on our parts to fulfill our wishes and our wants ahead of anything else.

If we look back at a later date, we realize how small and now narrow our vision was at the time. Hopefully, as we further our education, our world and the scope of our life begins to grow.

Another very important point is all the news that deals with other planets, living on the moon or Mars, and extra-terrestrial visits by aliens to earth.

It is no wonder that many of our young people, whether through drugs, TV programs, etc., want to leave this world to plan a course of their own "somewhere out there." The simple explanation is that they are seeking a surreal experience.

They don't want to make their way in our world because of the hardships and disappointments they would face. They see the world not with themselves in it but out of it. There is no ownership by these people that they are here to work with others to produce a better world for their families, children, and grandchildren.

I am a Catholic counselor. My immediate thought is what would Christ say about all of this? The first crucial fact in Christ's life is that He left eternity, with all of its glory, and came to earth, a problem-filled place, to save us. He came to bring God into our tearful hostility-filled world. That was not an escape. We are each put on earth to help others and ourselves gain heaven. That is how Christianity views the world.

Ronda: For a convert from an atheist background to belief in God and eternal life, I moved from a totally horizontal view of the world to a vertical one.

Bob: One person, who sees him- or herself as an agent of change, can change the whole world.

Ronda: For example, a builder of houses is graced with an insight into the possibility of solar heating. He or she works on this. It is experimented with, and the heating and cooling of homes is eventually changed for millions.

Bob: Most great movements have started with one person. The initial question should really be how does God see me in the world, and what are the graces He has really given to me to start His journey? Notice, it is not my journey, but His journey.

Ronda: I have noticed that some people in service jobs such as cleaners, care-givers, cashiers at super-markets are marvelously friendly. They actually smile sincerely at everyone who comes by or needs their help. They actually ask, "How are you?" as if they wanted a real answer.

Now, they could be defining themselves by the work they do, but God could have given them this work partly with the purpose of their expressing loving kindness to others.

Bob: Good examples. Now, what could upset the delicate balance between our self-definition and God's plan. Quite simply, it is the individual autonomy that people pursue and covet in their lives. If this sounds familiar, it is found in the Bible. "Thou shalt have no other strange gods before me." How we see ourselves on this earth is not something we see, but something we detect.

Ronda: So, to use the example above, we may only gradually come to see from what others tell us that we are valued very much for the loving kindness we show in our even passing conversations with them.

Bob: That happens when one stands on the same ground as in childhood, but now in adulthood everything is different. The experience of life to that point only indicates how much you need other people. During my recent stay at a convalescent home after an operation, I came to observe how the aides cared so much for their patients. They were not highly paid, but clearly they were dedicated to helping people, including me, get well. It was probably the most menial job in the home, but clearly one of the most important. And I was totally dependent on them for my comfort and cleanliness, and they were the first people I called upon for help.

In general, as we age, our bodies may be less muscular, or our hair more gray, and our walking less sure. Gradually, we may come to realize

that we are not autonomous but totally dependent on God for everything!

Like Jesus and Lazarus, it is only God who can
raise you from the dead. Like Jesus in the garden
of Gethsemane, God may very well take you
down a path you'd rather not take. It is a humbling, overwhelming path, but it is the path that
God and only God can choose for you.

For the Reader:

Take the time to trace your journey of self-
definition from childhood dreams through adult
life? Does greater dependence on God feel scary
or more of a humbling awareness of God's love.

_____

_____

_____

_____

_____

_____

_____

_____

_____

_____

_____

_____

_____

_____

_____

_____

_____

_____

_____

_____

_____

_____

_____

_____

_____

_____

_____

_____

_____

_____

_____

_____

_____

_____

_____

_____

_____

_____

Do I Learn from the Moment?

Bob: In fact, we can learn much from the moment. We are not guaranteed any more time in life on this earth than this moment.

A moment can give our lives a new direction. I am a firm believer in synchronicity; that is, at the right moment, I will be directed in a sometimes totally new way.

Ronda: As in I might meet a person who is starting an enterprise that I have never imagined might become my future work.

Bob: It comes to us in our awareness where the mind sees the same reality in a totally different way.

Life is built on a series of moments. Some can really stand out – your spouse that you spotted for the first time, your first baby's face looking back at you, and your child going off to college for the first time. But did I learn from the moment, or put another way, what was this particular moment meant to teach me?

Ronda: For a single person, this might be a call to a life as a missionary or from studying engineering to becoming a journalist.

Bob: The simple answer is that the moment exists to teach you everything. It has all the qualities of a kaleidoscope, with new knowledge appearing no matter at what angle you look. The most important point is that you are suddenly a micro-world. Each moment is a time-capsule with lessons that no other moment can give.

Ronda: For example, during my teen years and early adulthood as an atheist excited about exploring love through love affairs, I certainly felt a sense of the attractiveness of different young men. However, when I fell in love with my husband to be when I was already a Catholic, I saw in my future spouse's eyes his unique soul in an instant.

Bob: When the pregnant moment is viewed in such a way, an explosion of new information comes rushing into our minds. We have to be true to ourselves and to the moment and let this laser beam of information alter our activities completely, if that is what we are called to do.

Ronda: Hold on a moment! I would make a distinction between big moments that involve a good change and others that might be the result of some evil spirit urging us on to a decision that will harm ourselves and others. An example I witnessed years ago was a woman with small children thinking she was told by the Holy Spirit to leave her family in the US and go to Jerusalem to convert the Jews! More common still were many who were convinced that by the year 2000 the end of civilization was imminent so forced their families to move to small farming communities.

Bob: It's important to always distinguish whether the gate is of our making or God's making. Before you open the gate, be sure that it is from God.

Ronda: How? Many people find such discernments very complicated.

Bob: Before someone opens the gate, he or she should ask whether this is really something he or she wants to do or something God is calling him or her to do. Is the problem for these misguided people you just referred to the issue of presumption? One ought to hold the seeming truth of the moment in prayer before making life-changes based on it.

Ronda: I have found asking the advice of mentors and counselors is extremely helpful.

Bob: Right now, I want to explore those moments which really are from God and their effects on the recipient.

The moment is the gate opening up to insights never imagined. What do we do with this tsunami of information compressed in this fragment of time? What we should do is open ourselves completely to this brand new awareness and let it open our consciousness to new ways of operating. This takes supreme honesty with yourself to turn thought into action.

In the lives of some people, this moment has the force of multiple energies. When we read about Mother Teresa of Calcutta suddenly deciding to serve the poorest of the poor in Calcutta, India, or of St. Paul on his way to Damascus suddenly converted from persecutor of Christians to a leader of Christians, we have to acknowledge that a major change has occurred.

In our own lives, the change will rarely be that dramatic, but still it can be enormous for us.

The moment can be like a compressed atomic bomb, which suddenly releases all of its potential power to be actualized in the mind of this person. What then is this powerful moment? It really is a ray of God's grace freely given to someone to give help to the community or the world at large. Also, like a comet that streaks across the heavens, the moment is destined to go on until it has accomplished all of its objectives.

I recently had an operation on my pancreas to remove a cyst that was lying on it. After the operation, I had my moment of all moments when the surgeon's nurse called me to say, "You are completely cancer free." That moment was God's special present to me, which I will thank Him forever and ever. This joyous information opened up for me the many opportunities with my family and allowed my writing to continue to grow and to get even closer to God.

For the Reader:

What moments in your life so far have been have led to a dramatic change in either your life or your inner mentality?

_____

_____

_____

_____

_____

_____

_____

_____

_____

_____

_____

_____

_____

_____

_____

_____

_____

_____

_____

_____

_____

_____

_____

_____

_____

_____

Do I Know You, My God, Occasionally or Always?

Bob: This question requires great honesty. I believe the correct answer for most of us is occasionally. Why should that be when we know and proclaim that there is a God who loves us and only asks that we love Him back? Are most of us sometimes prodigal children who only acknowledge our father when we are in dire straits?

Recently, a visiting nurse came to my home to examine me after a pancreas operation. One of the questions she asked me was: "Are you homebound?" Of course, I am homebound to a certain extent, but I am not homebound with respect to my communication with God. I can talk to God at any time or any place.

God talks to me when I stop and have focused listening. I don't mean loud words on a mountain top as He did with Moses. He may whisper to me or use words which He places in my mind to tell me what His direction is for me at this moment.

Ronda: God speaks to me in my heart without loud words such as, "Ronda, stop scheming to avoid suffering!"

Bob: We know God is always available; we know He is our creator and our savior. What is our disconnect?

Here are some possible answers:

a) We are too busy with our so-called important projects. As a friend of mine said: "too many oars in the water." There is one major project in our lives – to talk with and be close to our God. In the U.S., many people have a compulsion to fill every minute with activity. Perhaps it reflects a fear of being alone with your own thoughts.

No wonder God can't talk to us. He wants to talk, but sometimes we don't want to reciprocate.

b) Do we really believe there is a being called God who is all powerful and all-knowing? Why wouldn't we want to talk to Him? But our tendency, especially in the U.S. society, is to fall back on our own abilities and own minds.

c) Our technology has subverted our spirituality. We may acknowledge God intellectually, but I am talking about a different mode of communication. I am talking about devotion, which implies an emotional attachment between ourselves and God. What we are talking about here is a relationship. This is not just a primary relationship. We are talking about a holy, in fact, *the* holiest relationship possible. If we believe, it is the most important conversation of our day. This is a conversation with the Holy of Holies, never to be trivialized. The real problem here is we have everything backwards. The first and most important activity of the day is to talk to Jesus and seek His guidance. All other relationships are a very distant second. I find that talking to God and seeing his handiwork in my life is second nature to me. As I view the intricacies of the world, I cannot help but praise Him and His glory.

Ronda: Possibly, you are thinking that you are much busier than Bob, a retired professor. Here is an example though that I have never forgotten. I had a woman friend with seven children who loved to pray. She got the older ones to watch the little ones while she spent an hour a day in meditation on Scripture in the bedroom.

Bob: I realize that many people don't talk to God all day. Why? The reason that they don't is because of what I call "snares." We are confronted with so many choices every day that talking to God is the last thing we do or don't do at all.

But, as with St. Augustine and his mother, St. Monica, who prayed for him to return to the Church, he came back to the faith and in doing so gave us his book *The Confessions*. This is essentially an apology to God for not talking to Him and engaging Him in conversation, an outpouring to God of his thoughts and feelings.

Let us also remember that Christ in the garden before His passion, shed not beads of sweat but droplets of blood, knowing what He was to do for mankind. This a debt we can never pay back, but we can give Christ our most precious gift, our time. When time becomes eternity, the rewards will be great because we can never outdo God.

For the Reader:

Consider examining your daily schedule and seeing where you might find more time for prayer. Some pray on their commuter trip to work. Some rise half an hour earlier or plan a quiet half hour before sleep.

_____

_____

_____

_____

_____

_____

_____

_____

_____

_____

_____

Are Things More Important than People?

Bob: What a strange question! Of course, we care for people more than things. Our Judeo-Christian heritage is the basis for this view.

This is what we profess as a nation, but is this how we live each day? That is the paradox of life in the U.S. Our real goal in the U.S., especially as seen on social media, is to want more and more and more things. Why? Because this is how some of us keep score within our families, with our neighbors, and especially with the people we work with each day.

We don't talk about people as much as we talk about things: new cars, new homes, new trips, new diamonds, etc. I believe the underlying issue is we are afraid that people won't love us, so we present to them an unending list of our accomplishments. We can then say to ourselves I'm better off than they are. What we are really saying is I'm so afraid of failure or criticism that I must have these things to protect me, to act like a talisman.

Ronda: In my sphere, giving talks to groups that included many women who did not have Ph.D.'s and had not written many books, I found that one might come up to me afterwards and start her question with this comment: "I'm not accomplished as you are, but..." To which I would ask how many children she had. If she said five, I would reply: "Well, I had four miscarriages besides my three on earth...which of your children, who will live forever in eternity, would you substitute for a published book which will one day be in an incinerator!"

Bob: The fact is that when we put things before people, we are putting the cart before the horse. We can get along without a lot of things, but we can't get along without relationships.

Ronda: You don't mean, of course, basic necessities, or that our ideal should be to become street people, do you?

Bob: Of course, I don't mean necessities. But back to my point, I am aware that relationships can be very messy. That's because they are part of the ebb and flow of life. They are also the elixir of life taking us to new heights about ourselves and other people. They provide constant teachable moments that help us to grow.

Our possessions are only extensions of ourselves. What we desperately need is to have others cross-pollinate us mentally, emotionally, and physically. Without relationships, we slowly disintegrate because to live is to reach out to others.

I was recently talking to a friend of mine who is involved in finances. We both came to the same conclusion – wealthy people are not necessarily happy and, therefore, they continue their journey to accumulate more. This is where relationships come to our aid. Happiness is within. Relationships are within. Accumulations are without.

There is another aspect to this issue of things vs. people. Whatever trinkets we accumulate on our earthly passage are just part of the role(s) we play on earth. But roles are no more than the kind of clothes we put on every day. They are not our core self. This brings to mind the difference between illusion and reality, which compose the yin and yang of all our lives.

At the time of our death, only the core self remains. All other possessions are shed in an instant! Therefore, our roles come to a screeching halt and cease to exist. These possessions mean nothing. What most people don't see is that possessions are the illusions of our lives. The only true barometer or measure of our lives is the relationships we have had and the good we have done for people. This is the true measure for the person vis-a-vis eternal life.

Ronda: A humorous example of my own is that I used to feel depressed at airports. I finally realized it was because the passing people would see me as an old hag instead of as Dr. Chervin with all these accomplishments. My role was not visible!

Bob: St. Francis of Assisi and St. Clare knew this all too well. They dressed and acted simply. Possessions were never an issue for them. In fact, Francis was able to personify this principle into a person – Lady Poverty. He wasn't just talking about living in poverty, although he and Clare did that, too. Rather, Francis saw through the externals that people present on this earth by specifically mentioning the spirit of poverty. This enables us to live rightly in the world but not be of the world.

A personal example: beginning in my teen years, I had to work hard to start to prepare for college. That meant only going with the basics and denying myself activities such as sports in High School, or mini-vacations, or skiing, etc. This meant a shedding of normal activities for the sake of a major goal. I think this mirrors in some way what St. Francis was talking about with regard to simplifying our lives.

Christ talked about the same thing with regard to pruning or shedding the "barnacles" we have accumulated in life. In fact, the Ten Commandments are the source of this letting go.

What does Christ say: "Forgive your enemies, love your mother and father, love your neighbor as yourself, etc."

There is always time to purify ourselves and to grow closer and closer to our God. Being poor in spirit is a distinct pathway, or, more precisely in Eastern thought, Christ is always the Way to eternal life.

For the Reader:

Make a list of the people in your life since childhood whom you treasure. Do you need to think about and talk about them more often than about things you have had or now have?

_____

_____

_____

_____

_____

_____

_____

_____

_____

_____

_____

_____

_____

_____

_____

_____

_____

_____

_____

_____

_____

_____

_____

_____

_____

_____

_____

How Long Do I Hold onto
Anger and Revenge?

Bob: My first response would be to ask who would want to hold onto anger and revenge?

Ronda: A frequent example of my own is that when someone disagrees with me and I am sure I am right, say, about abortion being wrong, I start yelling back at them. I will say something sarcastic such as, "Oh, you think the babe in the womb is just a clump of cells which might come out of the womb as a cat?" Then, if they don't shut up, I may take revenge further by telling my pro-life friends about how this person said this stupid thing.

Bob: A good example. These two commodities of anger and revenge are at the heart of physical, emotional, and intellectual problems. If we choose to hold onto anger and revenge, the end

91

negative result is totally on us. If we don't let them go, they are extremely toxic to our total being resulting in cancer, stomach difficulties, etc. In other words, such anger at people we disagree with if multiplied, including sarcasm and gossip, could have the power, if we hold onto them, to lead to death. How so? It seems as if the anger is outward, but it is as if the enemy lives within our own psyche and body.

Anger and revenge are directly tied to our perception of reality and a certain rigidity in how we solve or in fact don't solve problems. They are really born of a childlike emotional way of thinking, rather than an adult deliberation of how this situation can be solved.

Ronda: Instead of thinking of good responses to the pro-choice person's ideas, I am letting out my anger in sarcasm. I could instead patiently explain the stages of growth in the womb from conception to birth.

Bob: I would like to take this information and make it more concrete to see its full dimensions.

The first point I want to make is that hot anger and revenge are not part of our composed, resting self. In fact, when they show up, they are in control of us. This control can be in extremely destructive ways. We definitely are not in control of them.

For the sake of clarification for the reader, I would like to compare these two states of mind to something that I am very familiar with, namely, cigarette smoking. I used to do hypnosis to alleviate cigarette smoking. I had an 80% success rate in curing people of this very negative habit.

The one thing I want to emphasize is that anger, revenge, and cigarette smoking represent things we choose to do to ourselves. What I will say about cigarette smoking is that concretely the taking in of smoke, etc., can be seen. Obviously, the giving forth of anger and revenge can only be seen in a more abstract way. Hot sarcastic words and vengeful gossip are not visible like smoke, but that doesn't make them less toxic.

Let's take a very close look at cigarette smoking. When we are born, we go from our mother's womb, which is approximately 98.6 degrees, to the outside world of 70 degrees. This is a painful drop in temperature for this newborn, who is then given his mother's breast or bottle to pacify him or her. The child from that point on is orally fixated at birth. That means when we are in pain, we tend to go orally. When we use hot anger or revenge, which probably includes a lot of shouting on our part, we are telling someone they have crossed our boundaries. As in, how dare you contradict the truths that brilliant me believes? Each of these ways – cigarettes, anger, and revenge – share one thing. We have chosen a very toxic intervention to deal with life's problems.

Cigarette smoking obviously has tar and nicotine coursing through our arteries, veins, and especially our heart. That's why doctors ask us the question, "Do you smoke?"

In a quite similar physical way, anger and revenge put tremendous pressure on our bodily systems emotionally. The only difference here is that cigarettes take in negativity while anger and revenge spew it out.

Here is what all three of these reactions have in common – each action may not kill you today, but incrementally they may result in a premature death. Even if you, the reader, are a hot anger person but have lived very long, that doesn't mean it hasn't harmed you emotionally.

What they do represent are the end result of woundedness. We can't solve this situation by ourselves. As Christians, we need help from the one who was wounded repeatedly in His passion – Our Lord Jesus Christ.

He leads us to realize there is a different way in life. It is to offer up our pain in life in order to accept Christ's forgiveness. The life lesson here is that what we thought was so right was, instead, so wrong. Christ is standing at the crossroads of our lives always pointing the way.

For the Reader:

Do I Continue to Honor my Father and my Mother?

_____

Where do I Place myself, in Fantasy or Reality?

_____

Do I Love my Neighbor, my Children and my Grandchildren?

_____

Do I see Jesus as the Savior of the World?

_____

PROBLEMS OF OLD AGE

Fortitude

Ronda: From a year of trying out Assisted Living, I see that many, many elderly people from the age of seventy or older are faced with multiple possibilities of living situations and have a very hard time sorting out the pros and cons.

Do you, Bob Sizemore, as a counselor, have any over-riding principles about such decisions?

Bob: I believe that those of us who have reached aged seventy and beyond have heard, especially from Hollywood, that when our lives are coming toward a natural end, we will have the golden years to enjoy.

This idea is not only erroneous, but also dangerous.

Ronda: Ooooh! I didn't think I fell into that trap, but maybe I have, in subtle ways, such as imagining perfect Catholic assisted living communities where everyone would adore me and hang on my every word?

Bob: At a time when we have the opportunity to expand our world vision, many of us contract our vision and think only of the "great" days rolling up.

What I mean is that a person needs to act counter-culturally and continue to grow, and to produce the new chapters of their book of life!

Ronda: Yeah, sure! As in such jokes as this one: after a certain age I prefer a good bowel movement even to good sex!

Bob: Humor aside, Ronda, it is not healthy to fall back on old perceptions such as, "This is what life owes me, or was promised to me – a beautiful house, a wonderful spouse, great-grandchildren visiting frequently."

I am constantly amazed at the new people who enter my life every day with their very unique experiences. For example, what do I do when I meet someone who is a mirror opposite of me, which means someone who is usually gentle, yet I'm distrustful.

As I see it, I need to adjust my own experiences and outlooks to fit the issues that this person presents.

Ronda: Oh, Bob. That's fascinating. I run across this often in my own life.

So, give me an example of how you would become less distrustful in a concrete situation.

Bob: Older age is a different kind of golden years. Where have I been distrustful? For example, when I am buying a new large-priced item for our house, a stove, dishwasher…I am very distrustful at the point of the sale wondering how I can really trust what the salesperson is saying.

A different way of operating would be to trust that salesperson and realize that if this particular business is rated as honest, probably I could trust the seller.

Ronda: So, you are turning my question around from "Bob, Catholic counselor, tell me how to have a perfect old age?" to "How about a different perspective where you see old age as a time of growth in virtue for yourself?"

Bob: For example, I don't think it's good in old age to throw up one's hands often and claim I'm too old to try anything new.

Ronda: Oh, my gosh! I do this all the time, quoting to amuse people the famous joke:

"First I didn't want to leave my country.
Then I didn't want to leave my state.

Then I didn't want to leave my city.

Then I didn't want to leave my neighbor-hood.

Then I didn't want to leave my block.

Then I didn't want to leave my house.

Finally, I won't want to leave my bed!"

Bob: Oh, funny. I thought you would end with "Then I didn't want to leave my mind!"

Ronda: There is some truth, of course, in the fact that gradually in old age we become more limited, but…you seem to want to convey a different truth.

Bob: The truth is that in many cases we are not as limited as we think, but we have closed ourselves off from the stimuli that would continue to make our lives both interesting and challenging and productive.

Ronda: Okay. I had an interesting example. I was visiting a person who was wanting to declutter. At first I thought, I'm only a guest, and I shouldn't interfere to speed up such a process. But, gradually, since I was visiting for a long, long time, my host permitted me to take over some aspects of the process.

I found, to my enormous surprise, that getting out of my sedentary ways and running around decluttering actually gave me enormous physical energy and a sense of accomplishment!

Bob: What we should be doing in old age is cluttering up our minds with new ideas and stimuli. We should pick up a new book or engage in a new conversation with the goal of being open to new ideas.

Ronda: Oh, I've been doing that the last few years. Usually, I go through libraries at Catholic institutions I am near to and read lives of saints and biographies of good people. But, for the last few years I haven't had access to such libraries, so I go through the shelves of people I visit and pick out books about people I have never known anything about such as auto salesmen just at the time that cars came in and those with horses were sure it was a passing fad.

Bob: We are all extremely intricate individuals. Unless we make a point of reaching out to the stranger, we limit the world and conversations to mere formalities.

Ronda: I have a fantastic example. I was living at an assisted living facility right next to a Catholic Church. Here is an example of a totally unexpected conversation with a man who worked as a baker all his life. Here is what he said as I passed him in the dining room where the acoustics allow everyone present to hear every sentence anyone says:

"Ronda, here in this place all the women are dried up and ugly, but it's better than nothing!"

I replied after 10 minutes, "Well, this is a place where some of the men are old and rude, but it's better than nothing."

Quite an unusual back and forth for a retired philosopher professor!

Bob: We, for the most part, end up limiting ourselves by our decisions not to engage in conversations. We don't realize that a thought we might have shared with this person might have been a turning point for them in their lives.

Ronda: But what if the others around us are so borderline demented that most of what they say is totally irrational, as in a 97-year-old woman complaining bitterly that the administration of the assisted living facility doesn't let her parents come to visit her.

Bob: The fact that you stopped and listened to her probably did more good than you were aware of at the time.

For the Reader:

Can you find examples from your own life of being surprised at how good it is to try something new?

_____

_____

_____

_____

_____

_____

_____

_____

_____

_____

_____

_____

_____

_____

_____

_____

_____

_____

_____

_____

_____

_____

_____

_____

_____

The Depression and the Economy

Ronda: At the time we are writing this book of nuggets, we are still in Covid. While I know from reading about it that Covid hurt the economy greatly, I have no personal experience of such problems around me. So, tell me more about what you mean by the title of this topic, Bob.

Bob: This is a huge topic but one that has to be addressed, especially in these times. Regardless of your political persuasion, right now, with all the problems people face today in the U.S., I believe most people feel that their quality of life has diminished. America seems to have always been a country where folks think it important to always have more – more land, newest farm equipment, more luxurious vacations.

Ronda: Maybe because most of the people I know are elderly retired, I am noticing the opposite – middle class people who have millions of things in their houses and everything they need or even want.

Bob: I understand what you are talking about, Ronda, but I want to address more the felt sense of diminished wealth. The question is how do we approach that situation from a Catholic perspective?

The answer, to me, in this case, is not that we live the solution each day but live the question.

How do I face a daily life which requires that I come to terms with less not more in a country that has always promised me more? Examples could be having to sell the house with a large mortgage and live in a cheaper apartment. Only have one car for the family instead of two.

What it means to live a Christian life in one's later years with less money, less social life, less control, less mental capacity, and less physical health.

In other words, I believe we face a paradox in older age – we are forced to confront ourselves stripped of all the bells and whistles we have accumulated and rather confront a reduced lifestyle of what it really means to be a Catholic, a Christian.

The central point I want to make is we probably see this diminished life as a form of death, when, in actuality, Christ is calling us to new life in Him, to trust in Him in all things.

What I am saying is that there is tremendous opportunity in having less. The opportunity is that we are at a crossroads of choice – becoming less materialistic and much more spiritual as we slowly head towards our real life, our afterlife in heaven. As a secular Franciscan, I can think of no other saints who bring this point home more than St. Francis. His worldview was that he wasn't just in poverty, no, much more. He was confronting and living with Lady Poverty from whom he had so much to learn. Pain is the great teacher!

For the Reader:

Have you suffered from the economy in some ways? How have you accepted this as a Christian?

_____

_____

_____

_____

_____

_____

_____

_____

_____

_____

Diminished Status after Retirement

Bob: Roles in our Lives: We live in a highly competitive society. Many people will admit that they are probably moving faster in their work lives than they prefer. In fact, some parents may have to choose to spend more time at work than at home.

Ronda: You mean even with sleep time?

Bob: No. But this does produce sleep deprivation for many people. Stress is more rampant than ever before. What happens when this fast moving train of our lives stops and we find ourselves in retirement.

Ronda: Tell us about your experience of this.

Bob: In my own life, I suddenly found myself at age 75, no longer a teacher. Needless to say, teaching brought much happiness and adulation to my life. Now, I found myself at home trying to figure out what else I was good at or should pursue.

Ronda: Oh, since you used to be my crisis counselor, I always assumed that most of your time was spent in that occupation.

Bob: Not really. Teaching was always my main profession – sociology. While I first viewed retirement as a loss in my life, what it did do is propel me into counseling, spiritual direction, and writing, such as *The Franciscan Desert Pack: A Story of Interspecies Communication* (published by AuthorHouse, 2015).

What this taught me was that any problem I saw could be strictly in my perception.

Ronda: Years ago, I was living in Sedona, Arizona, and was at the Church with a group of devout men who were life-long golfers. They had bought condos on a golf-course, planning to spend all their elderly years enjoying their favorite sport.

After about three years of this, they become bored. And, they did something so wonderful, I am sure you would like to hear it. They put together all their know-how from previous jobs and built a Church in New Mexico for Mother Teresa's Sisters ministering there!

Bob: What your story about the golfers illustrates to me is that there is a God-given drive to continue with meaningful work but more so on the spiritual level.

Ronda: When I retired some five years ago from teaching at Holy Apostles College and Seminary where I met you, Bob, I was hoping to become a full-time contemplative, hopefully levitating on the ceiling Teresa of Avila style.

Far from that, when I saw I had too much time on my hands, I asked at the parish in Texas how I could help. It turned out that what was most needed was shredding! By law every Church has to shred, after three years, every donation envelope that has the address of the donor on it.

To my amazement I loved shredding! Why? Because it's a way to do something meaningless and get away from frantic anxious thoughts about my future.

Bob: How about now?

Ronda: I have had to shift away from the central position of authority as a professor, speaker, and writer. Instead, I find myself delivering nuggets of truth to people in passing or in social situations. Also, I help others write their books.

Bob: What is the Catholic answer to this change in our life-styles, given longevity?

The immediate answer to retirement is that we cannot play the roles that we have played all our lives.

Make no mistake, this is a severe jolt to our over-all self-image and to our physical well-being.

Added to that is the fact that our income may be cut in half in retirement, and we may have to begin the act of down-sizing to cope with this new reality.

Also, as we get older, our physical and mental health begin to slip as we make our way to even older age.

Usually, in one to five years, the people at work don't know us any more. New people have come on board.

We are eventually forced to shed old roles and take on new roles.

Ronda: One I often observe as a widow is that when a husband retires, he sometimes fills in the vacuum by becoming the domineering boss of his wife, previously queen of the house!

Bob: I was told that when Lyndon Johnson retired he went back to the farm and told his cows what to do!

For the Reader:

If you are a retired person reading this chapter, tell us about loss of status as you have experienced it. If you are not yet retired, do you have any ideas of other things you would like to be doing when you have all the time in the world.

_____

_____

_____

_____

_____

_____

_____

_____

_____

_____

_____

_____

_____

_____

_____

_____

_____

_____

_____

_____

_____

Growth is Still Possible?

Bob: We are eventually forced to shed old roles and take on new ones. What we come to realize, in time, is that our roles were not us, just the costume we got used to.

Ronda: You mean primarily job roles, not being a husband or wife or father or mother.

Bob: That's right. Therein lies the crux of the matter. In this situation, over time, we become aware that there is a deeper self, which now is free to emerge. We can get down to the base level of who we really are!

Isn't that what happened when Christ called Peter and Andrew? They put down their nets (roles) and followed Him to the kingdom of God.

Of course, many people are afraid to do this because they confuse their roles with real life.

Also, Christ offered the same opportunity to the Samaritan woman at the well. She kept talking about gathering drinking water (role), but He kept talking about eternal water, life-giving water for entering the kingdom. He then asked her to announce this to her friends and relatives.

These situations from the Bible indicate to us that we always have a choice; in fact, we are only a choice away from changing our future significantly.

Ronda: Beautiful, Bob. Now tell us how this pertains to your life after your retirement from college teaching.

Bob: When I retired from college teaching per se, I chose to go to Holy Apostles College and Seminary to apply for a position there. Little did I know that while teaching there was important, new key people became my clients in my other vocation as a counselor including you, Ronda. In meeting you, I met a woman who was both a teacher and a writer who complemented me completely. This encouraged me in my new role as a writer of novels.

Ronda: I have found that after retiring from teaching at Holy Apostles two former auxiliary occupations came into the forefront: running writers' groups and helping individual writers to complete their projects.

Bob: So, retirement can and should mean new life.

It can especially be a new life with yourself. There awaits us a new awareness of who we really are in God's eyes! As a friend of mine said: "Be kind to yourself; you never met a nicer person!"

Ronda: Oh, sure. But, in my case, a big negative emerged. Without the platform of the classroom, the part of me that thinks about ideas incessantly turned instead of obsessive thoughts about absolute trivia.

For example, I can spend hours trying to figure out whether mopping the dirty floor is an obligation or merely a convention of stupid housekeepers!

Bob: Whatever we choose to do is what we choose to do with our lives. If we choose to deal with trivial matters, we have the possibility of reducing our lives to minors rather than majors. It's not so much in the cards that we're dealt but in how we choose to play them. If you play them from weakness, you get trivia.

For example, the mop may very well paradoxically represent the pen you should have in your hand to write the next novel.

In the same vein, for once in our lives, we have an opportunity to shed old perfectionistic tendencies. These usually stem from childhood and our parents' admonitions to "only get A's in school," or "only be the best."

This is a particular cross that firstborns and type A's (people who are driven toward success) carry their whole lives. They can't slow down or relax—even "when" the success is only fleeting and they take on another goal.

What they really needed was to hear from their parents, "I love you for who you are, not what you do."

These are the people who enter older age with frayed nerves, ulcers, heart attacks, and high blood pressure. When things slow down in older age, as they must, they find they have been leading a mechanistic existence, not a human existence.

Christ has a different message. He talks about going inward, not outward. The desert saints were seeking this as well as the Eastern Rite Catholic Churches.

If we really enter our inner life, we may hear Christ talk to us in a faint inner voice, saying, "It's time to come back to your true home."

Ronda: I agree in part. I heard Jesus tell me after I retired: "Stop dog-paddling in the waves of life and let me float to the shore of eternity."

However, Bob, when sages say it is more important to be than to do, I really have to laugh. Can you imagine what a parent would think if the child took this seriously and sat in a corner meditating all day, refusing to go to school or do his/her chores?

Surely, what people mean by more being than doing is not that, but more time in quiet thought and reflection instead of constant achievement.

Bob: It's almost impossible for a child today to just be and not do. When you add up all our electronic gadgets and social media, you get a constant stream of auditory stimuli. So, then, when does a child get in touch with his/her inner self at all?

For the Reader:

If you are an older reader what did you relate to in the theme of Bob Sizemore of this nugget? If you are younger, can you fantasize in a good way about any new options for retirement?

_____

_____

_____

_____

_____

_____

_____

_____

_____

_____

_____

_____

_____

_____

_____

_____

_____

_____

_____

_____

_____

_____

_____

_____

_____

Mourning

Bob: As I was going through Ronda's and my pages of writing, it occurred to me that now was the time, before I continued any further, to bring up this very important subject of mourning.

What can we mourn for? Just about anything will do. From our childhood, it might be a lost pet. Next, from our adolescence, it might be a lost first love that we continue to hold onto for the rest of our lives. From our early adulthood, it might be a famous singer or movie star who has died. As a much older adult, it could be a spouse that suddenly died, or died long ago. It could also be a school mate from childhood who has suddenly died. What is even more difficult is a close family member who has suddenly been taken away from us.

Ronda: In my case, the most terrible death was that of my son of twenty years old by suicide.

The next most terrible, but expected, was the death of a daughter at fifty-seven years old from lymphoma and then a blood clot.

Bob: The big question is, what do we do? I had my maternal grandmother, Mabel, die when she was 78 years old, which I did not expect at all. I can visibly remember my roommate from Providence College taking me to the train station and the long, lonely ride back to New Haven to be with my family and dead grandmother one more time. Just writing about this situation brings back a flood of sad memories because I was so close to her and the spirituality she taught me.

More recently, I lost a very close friend, whose name was Lucian. He died in his sleep. He and I would converse about the 'old days' when our grandfathers used to go hunting together. Most especially, we would talk about our grandfathers as larger than life figures. I think of him always as a brother, whose kinship was very close to me.

Let me say that mourning can apply to a lot of people and things. The more we think of them and grieve, the greater opportunity we give them to remain our friends, hopefully in heaven.

Even Jesus was deeply affected by mourning when one of his best friends died whose name was Lazarus. When Jesus went to visit Lazarus' family, Lazarus was already dead and lying in a tomb wrapped up in burial clothes. Jesus cried! The family asked why He didn't come sooner and use His powers to keep Lazarus alive?

Jesus, knowing Lazarus would die, deliberately delayed coming because He wanted the situation to serve as an example for His own death and resurrection. When Jesus was ready, He called for Lazarus from the tomb, and Lazarus came out still wrapped in his burial cloth and very much alive.

Ronda: I got enormous hope for my adult children after their death from different signs that they were saved and I would one day see them again. (My book *Weeping with Jesus*...details the grieving and eventual hope in the case of my son, Charlie.)

Bob: Of course, today, in our high-powered society, people don't want to mourn or mourn too much. What the average person doesn't realize is that we are layered people who need to mourn through the deepest layers of our lives. Then, and only then, can we move forward. If we try to short circuit the process, we may pay a heavy price in mental depression, emotional instability, physical ailments, and addictions of all types.

Ronda: In the case of my daughter's death, I expected to cry as much as I had with the death of my son twenty-five years before. However, instead, I became numb. I attributed the lack of tears to the long period of seeing her with brain death in the hospital and experiencing that her soul seemed to be ten times "bigger" than her dying body.

But, during the last two years since her death, I have felt much more depression and emotional instability and a greater addiction to picking my fingers.

Bob: What I have learned through my practice is that mourning is a question of "pay me now" or "pay me later." When you extinguish the emotional fall-out by mourning, you may also avoid a broken heart and high-blood pressure, hyper-sensitivity, etc. To mourn now, as long as you have to, is the best life-long investment you will make in your whole life.

Of course, when you consider the mind-body connection, the need for mourning becomes that much more apparent. We all have grown up with the help of family members and friends to become who we are. To have one of those supports taken away from us is a stress that is very hard to deal with.

If we do mourn sufficiently, we at least begin to heal the wound that has left us less than who we were. When in doubt, mourn and pray even more for the person you knew and will know again probably in heaven.

For the Reader:

It may help you to write here about your whole relationship with a loved one who has left this earth. Then, to pray fervently for that person's salvation.

_____

_____

_____

_____

_____

_____

_____

_____

_____

_____

_____

_____

_____

_____

_____

_____

_____

_____

_____

_____

_____

_____

_____

_____

_____

_____

_____

_____

_____

_____

_____

_____

_____

_____

_____

_____

_____

_____

Deeper Life in the Church

When many of those we loved the most are on the other side, Masses for the Dead are especially valuable. Meditate on ways that will help you maintain your relationship with those you love who've passed away.

_____

_____

_____

_____

_____

_____

_____

_____

_____

_____